My Toolbox Doesn't Like Me

A Selection of Poems

by

Sam Steele

First published in 2014 by
For The Right Reasons
(Charity no. SC037781)
Printers & Publishers
60 Grant Street, Inverness

British Library Cataloguing in Publication Data.
A catalogue record of this book is available
from the British Library.

ISBN: 978-1-910205--37-2

Cover design by Andy Ure

Forward

Sam Steele was born in Ontario, Canada where he lived for 10 years. He immigrated to the UK with his family in 1975 and in the next quarter century he emigrated a further 4 times. As a result Sam is thoroughly mid Atlantic in culture and accent.

Sam served in both the Canadian Armed Forces and the Royal Air Force for 20 years. He saw service in the Falkland Islands, Croatia, on the Sarajevo Air Lift, Air Operations Iraq, operations supporting the Former Republic of Yugoslavia, in Rwanda in 1994 and the Gulf War in 2004 and for a short time in Iraq after hostilities ceased. He retired from military life in 2007 and now runs a B&B in the Highlands of Scotland.

Sam started writing poetry in 1992, when as a Flight Commander in the Falkland Islands he had to give leaving speeches in the form of a poem. Since then he has moved from stories of mishap and amusement to ones of love, heartache, war, cancer, history, garlic and anything else that amuses him, that he finds uplifting, is thought provoking or that just plain bugs him.

Acknowledgments

My thanks to the team at *For the Right Reasons* for tolerating my haphazard and lengthy method of getting this book ready for publication. To Andrew Ure for designing the cover. To all the proof readers who spotted the numerous glaring flaws and tweaked the tiniest detail. To Peter and Danny, from CLIC Sergeant and Poppy Scotland respectively, for supporting the book launch. For the mixed gang at the Sunset Café whose positive feedback to my poems has spurred me on to actually get this book published. To Allison, my Partner in Rhyme for her advice and her support for various poetry related projects. To my children who tolerate my hobby including being dragged to the Sunset Café on a Saturday evening without which these poems would just be fading scraps of paper in the rarely looked at folder.

Dedicated to all my children

Contents

Alternate Five-a-Day

Computers

B.O.G.O.F

Fast food - I like the eating, not the buying

Coughing, Sneezing, Snuffling, Wheezing

Five Word Forecast

I Don't Like My Toolbox, My Toolbox Doesn't Like Me

I Hate Brussels Sprouts!!!

Iron man

Jazz

The Life of a Leaf

Littorally Majestic

My Trip to the Osteopath

Aurora Borealis

Punch Drunk

The Silent Killer?

Smothered Heart

Some Little Love Poems

There are Plenty Of States in the US

Think

It's the Thought That Counts

The Tick

The Unknown Truth

The Ultimate Box of Chocolates

Walking the Dog

Up or Down - Who Cares?

The Weekend

What's Your Special Day?

When I'm 92

The Yuletide Rush is Over

You Don't Get to the Moon Watching Soaps

Alternate Five-a-Day

Doctors like to have their say and make us all eat five-a-day
What we shouldn't, what we should, all to make our body good

With healthy body we're not complete, emotions we must also treat
To help you truly feel alive, here's your second daily five

HOPE each day that right succeeds, though good is never guaranteed
If hope is gone, the future too and then you'll turn a little blue

TRUST is crucial in the end, so trust a colleague, trust a friend
Rarely you'll feel malcontent. Trust 99.9%

LEARN from everything you can, 'cause you ain't got a perfect plan
A bad decision lands a blow. What made it bad? What you don't know

SMILE when're you see a face. It's like a hug without embrace
A smile's infectious have a go and see how far you make it grow

LOVE in heart and love in soul, loathing never makes you whole
Love your job, your kids, your wife. If there's no love then there's no life

If you do this without remiss the world around will blow a kiss
This won't bestow you fiscal wealth, but boy will you feel inner health

1

Computers

How would we live without them? They are good for many things
They make our life much better and so many joys they bring
But they are moody and expensive and a pain to have around
But we can't exist without them, we are intimately bound

There's a lengthy start-up process when first they come on line
I've no idea what happens but it's part of their design
They do lots of preparations or they cannot operate
So just have a cup of coffee, cause you're gonna have to wait

If you want to keep them running it can sometimes be quite tough
Cupboards of consumables, a myriad of stuff
Toner, cleaner, special wipes, lots of stuff that need a cable
And of course once you have got one you'll need a special type of
table

They are infinitely complex. It's a mystery how they work
Don't press the proper button, they can simply go berserk
I asked a friend and expert and I'm told it's all my fault
That if for no good reason all communications halt

An industry surrounds them and a media machine
The paper shop sells many kinds of glossy magazines
Devoted to the topics of their size and style and speed
And articles to help you through their every kind of need

Years ago without one I got by, but it is true
I'd be wholly lost without one and would wonder what to do
So if it gets a virus I'm left helpless, in a daze
I can't manage life without one; it's so hard in many ways

They can be moody and expensive and a pain to have around
But we can't exist without them, we are intimately bound
Sometimes she's so annoying that I simply want to shoot her
But enough about the missus, let's talk about computers

B.O.G.O.F

On Monday I went shopping, but when I saw the price.
I thought the thing expensive, even at a pound a slice.

Tuesday I was horrified, when the label I did see.
The price had doubled, 2 pounds each. Buy One, Get One Free.

They caught my eye on Wednesday, sitting in the bargain trough.
At just a pound the sign declared, that's 50% off.

The maths is fairly simple, if you do a quick compare.
I cannot see the saving, that the flashing signs declare.

Monday it's expensive, and then the next 2 days,
The price per slice is just the same, despite what you may say.

I don't like your style, your sneaky tricks, I'm not stupid, I can see.
My pound goes where it's needed. To my favourite charity.

BOGOF !!!

Fast food

I like the eating, not the buying

I'm feeling a little bit peckish
My stomach growls *'I want to eat*
Forget about salad or hummus
I want something that's loaded with meat'

So I go for my favourite burger
Though often it's been a dead loss
As service is not a high standard
And that makes me a little bit cross

I stand in a queue and I wonder
Why the counter has six tills that could work
But five staff that appear to do nothing
Just one youth who's acting as clerk

This kid by the till in a hair net
Has a 'Why do I have to work?' smile
The effort to order my burger
Seems to cramp his teenager style

Go large on the meal? Apple pie sir?
A side order? Some fries? And what drink?
Eat in our out of the restaurant?
Is that all? **I don't know, I CAN'T THINK!!!!**

When this verbal grilling is over
They put the meat on the grill out the back
Why can't there be burgers there waiting
And not metres of empty food racks?

They never prepare for the order
When it comes it seems such a surprise
Surely they must have an inkling
They only sell burger and fries

When I've paid *I* have to start working
Fetching beverage and ketchup and stuff
I guess queuing and paying and waiting
Aren't anything like hard enough

Now I'm one who likes extra green pickles
Others put the lettuce on hold
But never request special orders
Cause everything ends up stone cold

The staff find them tough to keep track of
When it's busy they cause much dismay
And why should they slog any harder?
There's no tips and it's minimum pay

You might get no sauce on your burger
For each portion of fries you see three
You pay for some nuggets but get none
Or tomatoes where your pickle should be

When it comes I munch it with gusto
I slurp on a drink that's all ice
I chomp on the thin cut potatoes
And conclude that mostly it's nice

But the work doesn't end, I must clean up
My tray to the bin I must bring
Minimum wage looks quite peachy
Cause what I do does not earn a thing

Fast food is the name it's been given
Whether food is still something to test
And the time that it takes to get service
Means clearly the 'fast' is in jest

It's just burgers and fries and a cola
Each prepared on a custom appliance
Can they not make it slicker and quicker?
It's a burger, it ain't rocket science

I've been ordering fast food for decades
In fact since fries were a nickel
And it's sad to report I'm still waiting
For my burger with extra green pickle

Coughing, Sneezing, Snuffling, Wheezing

There's a cooty on a handle and this cooty sits unseen
Maybe eighteen hours later you touch what's still unclean

Infection on your finger surprise, surprise, surprise
You help the critter get a hold, through mouth, through nose, through eyes

Exposure plus just 16 hours you start to feel the heat
The only thing to do right now retreat, retreat, retreat

A tiny, tiny virus of two hundred kinds in fact
Has taken a position in your respiratory tract

Coughing, sneezing, snuffling, oh happy happy day
Baton down the hatches a cold is on its way

Misery, dejection, sore nose, sore throat, sore chest
Ten days you have to suffer an unwelcome little guest

Fever, sputum, mucus, come back again, again
Sore throat, wheezing, ear ache and multi coloured phlegm

Pills can't fight the virus. Pills cannot interfere
It crushes every kind of pill and still it perseveres

You do not feel the virus, you feel symptoms of disease
So only take some medicine to get relief from these

Take rest, take drinks, take time off work, take yourself to your bed
And surface some days later with a clear and happy head

At this point take some action to keep viruses away
Wash and wash more often to keep the colds at bay

Don't rub your eye, don't rub your nose or lick your unclean thumb
And to the oh so common cold you're less likely to succumb

Though common by nomenclature it doesn't feel put down
It's called coronavirus because it wears a crown

Kings and Queens have caught them. Sultans, Pharaohs too
If it's good enough for Ramases then it's good enough for you

Five Word Forecast

Hey Met Man! You don't need a fancy degree
To spout what you spout every night on TV
Why spend years at Uni learning to speak
Weatherman waffle and Gobbledy Greek?

It's all just a ruse, a great fictional tale
With fantasy words like force nine Beaufort scale
Anomaly, millibar, unstable air
Katabatic, occluded. Oh, I despair

El Nino, advection, chinook or synopsis
Or Altocumulus lenticularis
Isobar, jet stream, inversion and squall
I've checked them on Google they mean nothing at all

All that's important is the clouds for the day
Are they light, are they dark, or medium grey?
You can spilt them in two, by their size, namely these
L W F Os and B B R Bs

The ones that we like, when the wind doesn't blow
Are what you should call L-W-F-Os
They are small, bright and lovely and blaze in the sun
An apposite name 'Little White Fluffy Ones'

The B-B-R-Bs are the large scary clouds
That makes us all wet and can be really loud
Just like Babe Ruth they're a bit of a slugger
B-B-R-B is 'Big Black Rainy Bugger'

I yearn for a forecast not wordy or long
The more that you say means the more you are wrong
Distil it right down to the simplest yet
"White clouds. You'll see sun", or
"They're black. You'll get wet"

I Don't Like My Toolbox
My Toolbox Doesn't Like Me

I've decided I don't like my toolbox, 'cause my toolbox just doesn't like me
I want to be friends with the contents, but somehow we just don't agree
They have their own spot in the garage; I oiled them and treated them nice
But over the years I've discovered all they want is a blood sacrifice

My Saw has got teeth made for cutting, though to wood it does almost no harm
But give it a push on the handle; it cuts most of the veins in my arm
My Hammer's allergic to metal, which I think is a little bit dumb
But since nails are what it likes hitting, it does, but only my thumb

Spanners are the devils invention 'cause there's plenty on hand I can choose
But no matter which one that I pick up it's always some flesh I will lose
If slightly too big I still use it, it slips and I scrape lots of skin
The next ten I pick are too little, I get mad and I punch the wall in

The Spirit Level could be quite useful if I could drink from the spirit inside
But it's a foul tasting concoction I was reckless one day so I tried
It's just one more hopeless invention. If short it is no use at all
If long it sticks out of the toolbox making unsightly marks on the wall

I once thought I mastered it's purpose. For the pat on the back I did wait
But the wife in her infinite wisdom advised me the pictures weren't straight
Up a bit, left, no, a bit more, a bit more, no, up on the right
It then fell from the wall broke a tea cup, my toe, two plants and a light

I feel quite in tune with the Hacksaw. The name is a little prosaic
But hack is the way that I use it, so it's quite onomatopoetic
I hack at the thing I want cutting. It might be quicker to wait till it rusts
And hack is the sound of my gasping when I breathe in a bunch of the dust

12

To fix little breaks in the kitchen there's a tube of Glue always to hand
And to get the glue where it is wanted, to squeeze is the simple command
But six holes all start oozing adhesive. If just one it would be so much better
And I wouldn't glue last Sundays paper to the arm of my wife's favourite
sweater

The Tape Measure is agoraphobic. It likes to stay inside its case
If you pull it out hard it defies you and returns to its spiral embrace
To hide from the light is so vital, that not for a second it lingers
It warp factors into the helix, as it goes it cuts two of my fingers

Apart from the tools that I've mentioned, there lurks several pieces of string
A Plumb Bob and Chisels for carving, I've no bodily use for these things
There are Screws and Nails by the dozen and everyone *just* the wrong size
But they stick to the tool I am using because each has become magnetised

But a recent addition I've noticed, the most useful thing by and by
I use it each time that I venture to give any contraption a try
It isn't a tool or instructions for what I'm about to install
It's simply the telephone number, of the doctor who's working on call

I Hate Brussels Sprouts!!!

Brussels are a cruciferous veggie
'Cause its flower is in the form of a cross
If you martyred each plant in a bloodbath
I'm one who'd rejoice at the loss

When your cousins are cabbage & broccoli
Kohlrabi, kale, collard greens
You think it would look at its gene pool
And not want to be tasted or seen

With the yuck of a whole head of cabbage
In something that's less than bite sized
It's no wonder to get kids to eat them
Takes a crow bar to get teeth unprised

I'm told that a good source of fibre
In this Lilliput cabbage is stored
It's just like some All-Bran at breakfast
Well that's not an enticing reward!!!

When you get to your granny's at Christmas
You excitedly stand at the door
But nearly collapse when it's opened
From the scent that out of it pours

14

They smell when they steam in the sauce pan
They pong when there're put on the plate
They stink when they sit in your stomach
There're a brassica marble I hate

You can boil, you can fry, steam or roast them
It does little to upgrade the taste
So here's the best way to prepare them
To minimise effort and waste

In a thin plastic bag you should store them
Maybe add a few brown onions skins
Your pea pods, your peeling and egg shells
And then throw the whole lot in the bin

The only thing worse than some Brussels
Is a sauce made from cold anchovies
If you served them together for dinner
You'd have Satan himself on his knees

I *Hate* Brussels Sprouts!!!

Iron man

My kids have a new superhero
A man who's a true gladiator
He can sort out a pile up with vigour
He's hot, but a smooth operator

A mountain of work matters little
As he knows just how to succeed
There's many a housewife that loves him
And he impresses with every good deed

Nothing can rumple this hero
Handling materials of every kind
With the power to burn you on contact
He can level whatever he finds

His side kick's as flat as a pancake
Braving searing heat right on the back
Three feet high at the tallest
And can tuck into the narrowest crack

The Ironman's gadget is streamlined
As heavy as a thick metal beam
Titanium coated and non-stick
With the power to make jets of steam

Ironman, gadget and sidekick
Are essential come laundry day
With steam at the touch of a button
And a handy wee knob for the spray

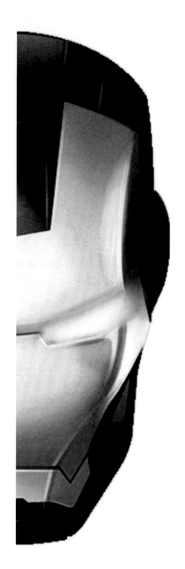

Oh they tackle the creases in cotton
On silk smooth the tiniest crinkle
Straighten the strands in a t-shirt
They flatten each cumbersome wrinkle

Handkerchief, table cloth, napkin
Corduroy, denim and flax
Once scrunched up and looking bedraggled
Ends up in the neatest of stacks

The husbands of old could lay concrete
And wield power tools like a drill
But this is the 21st century
And with it come different skills

Changing nappies and clearing up dinner
Work a grill or a vacuum or duster
Buying cushions that complement décor
Buffing wood to bring up the lustre

So perhaps he can't leap a tall building
And his fingers can't shoot balls of light
He can't stop a freight train by looking
But he can separate colours from whites

If married to this house keeping marvel
Who irons and cleans and cooks grub
Please remember to refresh his powers
With a pint and a mate, down the pub

Jazz

Each day I wake up feeling soulful
Each day I wake up feeling blue
Cause I have to go work in an office
When I'd rather be grooving with you

Some people like classical music
And others prefer rock & roll
Ain't nothing surpasses jazz music
Cause the beat lifts your heart and your soul

You're the only thing makes me feel lucky
When you're here I feel so much alive
There ain't nothing that makes me feel better
Than a few bars with a twist and a jive

Some people like classical music
And others prefer rock & roll
Ain't nothing surpasses jazz music
Cause the beat lifts your heart and your soul

So baby we should get together
I'll embrace you with both heart and hands
Cause heaven is a piece of jazz music
Played on you, my black baby grand

Some people like classical music
And others prefer rock & roll
Ain't nothing surpasses jazz music
Cause the beat lifts your heart and your soul

Inspired by Freya

18

The Life of a Leaf

I'm a leaf, I'm a leaf, I'm part of a tree
I'm strangely excited, but how hard can it be?
With 10,000 siblings, it's bound to be fun
Enthroned on a branch, as we bask in the sun

Winter
I lie in a twig, but I'm itching to grow
It's too blooming icy. I'm shrouded with snow
I'm frozen, unseen, I'm dormant and small
It's a wonder that there's any life there at all

I sit and I wait till the season is through
Like I've got to appease an upset Ghillie Dhu *
And the only respite that that is given to me?
The warmth that I feel when a squirrel has a pee

Spring
It warms up a bit and I feel like a stud
And people have taken to calling me Bud
Feeling a tingle at the end of my shoot
I'm eager and ready. Just show me the route

I then get a shock, because do you know what?
As Spring springs along I get juice up my butt
Still bitterly cold and I'm pumped up with sap
Which pushes me out, so I grow and unwrap

Then do you know what I am made to endure?
I'm forced to grow fast a few days to mature
I'm stuck where I am as I'm fussed to the tree
Some might think it fun but I tell you, not me

Now not to complain, though I'll be slightly blunt
My sartorial look is a natural affront
I see all the leaves, both the face and the back
Are green. I would surely do better in black

Summer

I try to be happy and a smile to maintain
I'm pushed by the wind, I get wet in the rain
Boys try to pick me and bugs nibble my tip
I really don't like it not one little bit

And there's the bad taste of the green chlorophyll
Change it to sugar is my role to fulfil
I clear the foul taste but whenever it suits
It gets sucked away and enjoyed by the roots

My 10,000 siblings? Oh, it's 20 times more
And every last one I have come to abhor
The 200,000 are on a crusade
To block all the light so I'm stuck in the shade

Autumn

So Fall then arrives and the clues in the name
This time of the year has a singular aim
To tree and to branch I must bid an adieu
But first I must change to a different hue

Sap sucked from my veins till I'm sickly and brown
I try to keep strong; I try not to fall down
And then there's a gale and I finally get shoved
Worn-out and aged. I'm now useless, unloved

The best chance I have, I would be lucky if
I stayed where I am till I freeze and go stiff
I'm flipped, spun and tossed of which I'm not very fond
I land in a ditch, in some mud or a pond

If raked in a heap I sit till I'm drier
A match on my stem. I'm fuel for a fire
More likely I'll lay till spring comes around
Then as it warms up I will rot on the ground

Dreams

The dreams that I had were all noble and grand
A tall maple tree is what I had planned
Regal and stately and resplendent and proud
My roots in the soil and my crown in a cloud

I'd be the whole tree, then one day perhaps
When tall, strong and wide some lumberjack chap
Would start off the process so I could be made
Into a book, or a chair, or a vast colonnade

But my short life is over. I've done what I could
And now I decay on the floor of the wood
But you should remember that every tree
Would just be a sapling if it wasn't for me

* In Scottish folklore the Ghillie Dhu is a faerie, a guardian spirit
of the trees

Littorally* Majestic

Surfing – there's nothing quite like it
A swim suit, my board and the swell
Nature my only companion
To the rat race I bid a farewell.

Waking early to surf at the sunrise
Alone at the dawns early light
There's me on a wave with a sunbeam
Sensing sun and the world reunite

I can't hear the sound of my printer
The growl of the planes up above
The TV, the news, or congestion
Just the pulse of the wave that I love

A wave that once lifted a tanker
An atoll once sensed its caress
It passed over a great pod of Orcas
Felt an albatross soar past its crest

From over the ocean it journeyed
In a time honoured pageant of power
Onward, ever onward
Every second, every minute, every hour

Together we glide 'cross the ocean
Like a Valkyrie till we hit ground
But we'll capture a moment together
As we seem inextricably bound

Once it senses the beach rising upwards
It knows that soon it will die
It summons up all of its power
And crafts a majestic good bye

Standing itself on its haunches
It's crest pointing up to the sky
For just a few moments it hangs there
Before it collapses and dies

SMASHING AND CRASHING!!! It's over
From the trough right up to the crest
The wave, the board and the surfer
Still united but now all at rest

Surfing – there's nothing quite like it
In another world you can dwell
For a moment I ride with Poseidon
A swim suit, my board and the swell

* Littoral – of or relating to the shore of a sea, lake, or ocean
(Collins Dictionary)

My Trip to the Osteopath

It's painful in the morning, which causes me distress
It hurts me when I do stuff. It hurts to simply dress

I look hunched in the mirror, clearly something isn't right
I'm off to get some treatment from a sadist wearing white

I hate his lobby posters of a body, minus skin
The eyes are always open, with a most perplexing grin

And as I sit there waiting, I hear a lots grunts and groans
How is this the dialogue as he tries to straighten bones?

I'm called into the treatment room, feeling like I've been condemned
The tyrant in a gleaming smock is pretending he's my friend

And there before me on display, suspended meek and solemn
I hope it's made of plastic. It's a vertebral column

I only had some back pain, now I'm feeling kind of ill
Is that what's left of someone who forgot to pay their bill?

The consultation's over, then I'm laid out on the bed
And this is when I panic, 'cause I know what's up ahead

He says "It's nothing scary". If that's really what he meant
Then how come I am folded up, twisted, rolled and bent?

His arms are wrapped around me and his hands are on my waist
Not even with my misses have I been this way embraced

My head is in my armpit. My toes and hip impact
My knee can touch my navel then he tells me to "Relax"

"Breathe in" he says "Yes that's good. I'll now do a slight adjust"
That's when I have to suffer a high speed lumbar thrust

A shot gun in the lobby!!! The waiting rooms in riot!!!
I'm told that that is normal and now it's gone all quiet

He tries again, machine gun burst. It's a full blown mutiny!!!
And then I come to understand. The sounds? They came from
me

He says to me "Oh that was good. In just one I got the lot"
We now need extrication from the human Gordian Knot

My body feels much lighter and I look a lot less bent
I can dress without it hurting. So I guess I'm glad I went

He's really very helpful. A superb osteopath
But I wish I could be treated with a gin and a bubble bath

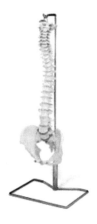

Aurora Borealis

The Aurora Borealis is flawless in the sky
It's there for pure enjoyment so never question why
I cannot do it justice, if you've seen it you will know
Mother Natures' best achievement is this nocturnal glow

She spied a stunning rainbow, arching tall, supreme
She captured all the colours before any had been seen
With this modest rainbow she worked into the night
Making iridescent curtains woven from the light

Suspended from the polestar, across the heavens laid
Floating shafts of colour in a silent accolade
Mother Nature hit perfection, in a profound, majestic way
It stuns your mind to see her stage this cosmic art display

They are perfection in the heavens, this tip to you I give
You can't die unless you've seen them, 'cause to see them is to
live

Punch Drunk

I'm feeling poorly. Please be sorry for me
It's like I just lost to Mohammad Ali
My head is split open, my stomach's in pain
And I don't want to ever feel this bad again

I went to a party not expecting to stay
I'll drink to be social then be on my way
When asked if I drink I said 'If you insist
One for the road. It's a shame to waste it'

'Why not, if it's free? I'll have one, then go
I'm not driving tonight and it's rude to say no
And the punch seemed to be quite innocuous stuff
But two was too many and three not enough

In the morning I woke with Beelzebub's breathe
My wardrobe exploded. I felt worse than death
My head in the bath and my feet in the sink
It hurt if I moved and it hurt just to blink

It wasn't my fault there's no need to get shirty
Some of the glasses they must have been dirty
The smoke in the room always makes me feel bad
Or it could be the virus that everyone's had

I never get drunk in under an hour
It must be the last one the garnish was sour
It wasn't my fault; it's no good blaming me
I only drank punch that was alcohol free (wasn't it?)

It was maybe the drink I finally relented
The juice in the punch had surely fermented
Or the mixer was something I'm sensitive to
That could be the reason I woke in the loo

I only had two drinks or perhaps it was more
Then I counted them up; it was close to a score
But my head it hurt worse then I don't know when
So I maybe had closer to three score and 10

If I drink without food I can sometimes get wired
I must be out of practice or I was just tired
The glasses were big yes that's where I went wrong
And the punch it was quite unpredictably strong

I'm feeling quite poorly. I know it's my fault
Make the pain go away and the spinning halt
And I promise myself no more grape, no more grain
So I never will have to feel this bad again

The *Silent* Killer?

I've heard it be called 'Silent Killer'
It stealthily stalks on its prey
And once it arrives at its target
It sits there with nothing to say

It silently waits to grow bigger
Doing little to tell you it's there
It leaches from everything near it
It grabs what it wants without care

It silently takes without giving
Offering nothing you want in return
To increase, to develop, to flourish
Is its singular driving concern

But I hear what it does in the silence
I hear each distraught question 'Why?'
I hear all the difficult breathing
I hear screaming, in terrified eyes

I hear the explosion and shrapnel
Of the lives that it rips all asunder
I hear the frustration and anguish
I hear the inaudible thunder

It hears not the coughing it causes
Nor feels the unbearable pain
It sees not the crippling impact
As it toils on its terror campaign

It might silently enter the body
And with stealth it dispenses its violence
But there's tears and there's pain and there's torment
It may kill, but it isn't in silence

Smothered Heart

Your heart wasn't nurtured with sunlight; you held it in a box
It couldn't express any feelings, you wouldn't allow it to talk
Any good heart feeling lovin, by nature it just wants to shout
But silent it lay in its chamber, choked by suspicion and doubt

Craving a wee touch of romance, hoping again you would try it
Instead it was fed meagre rations and that was a starvation diet
You dreamed of a prince in a castle but your heart lay alone in its tomb
Unable to reach its potential because of the self-imposed wound

Using armour and walls for protection, so you couldn't be hurt yet again
But these stopped all the love coming inward and held in the hate and
the pain
Though desperate to reach its potential, to the world your heart was
unseen
Only hope can imagine the future or knows just what should have been

In darkness, alone and abandoned, you've got what you've been
working for
No-one to journey through life with no-one will come through your door
Your heart might go on but it's weakened and so in a very short while
Your emotions will join with your spirit and live in eternal exile

Some Little Love Poems

Cupid is a rascal, I think that's fair to say
He fired a couple arrows from 500 miles away
So until I can embrace you in the comfort of my home
I hope you find some solace from a hug that's in a poem

Though my mind is always busy, my heart cannot forget
About the time when things turned round, the day we truly met
There are miles and lots of silence, but feelings don't subside
When sole mates come together, from however far and wide

Though your mind is always busy and your heart you've put aside,
Until your life is settled and the knots are all untied
Just remember someone's out there, who still holds a little flame
And cannot forget about you, 'cause the wind whispers your name

I felt a bit funny this morning
A tingling sense in my heart
Pressure and rate were all normal
But the temp had shot right off the chart

But then I received a text message
All at once it became so much clearer
It isn't a problem or worry
It's warming up because you're getting much nearer

There are Plenty of States in the US

There are plenty of states in the US
But just try to remember each name
The list will tax a good memory
And drive the forgetful insane

So here is a nice little ditty
To help you to think of each one
From the Keys right up to New England
Aloha to the Midnight sun

Let's start with an 'A' for Alaska
There's one at the end and the start
The same can be said for Al'bama
The place where you'll find Dixie's heart

There isn't a state with an 'E' sound
So off to the I 'Here we go'
Illinois and then to the Jones state
And finally there is Idaho

O is found in Oklahoma
A word that they must think is great
As it is the name of a city
And also the song of the state

The U has a single initial
Now let us go out on a wing
Not always a vowel to be certain
Who cares? 'Equal Right' Wyoming

The US is a fairly young country
And four of the names start with new
Hampshire and York and Jersey
As well as a Mexico too

M is a popular letter
Michigan, Montana, Maine
And the M with I and S letters
Again and again and again

There's a place with 'isle' in its title
But the real island state's in the sea
And between them there is Nevada
2 Dakotas and one Missouri

The green mountain state gets a mention
Connecticut and Kentucky
Florida, Kansas, Nebraska
Oregon and Tennessee

Of the states not already mentioned
Some have been named after men
The first was for lord De La Ware
And the keystone for one William Penn

Charles gets a couple of mentions
Carolina, both south and the north
Two Georges, such as the great founder
And George for the king before forth

And women of course get a mention
Let's detail two names that still stand
A westerly Queen with no off spring
And Marie who named Maryland

There's M plus another 12 letters
And an A to a Z back to A
And two states with only four letters
But each has three vowels to say

A 'solitree' star's in there somewhere
And a place with a Golden Gate Bridge
Colorado with all its straight borders
And the one with a blue mountain ridge

Nearing the end. Minnesota
The Pelican state makes it in
The second to last is R'Kansas
And finally of course Wisconsin

So that is the list start to finish
Some named and some just a clue
And should the states grow any bigger
I'll leave the new verse up to you

Think

When you send the boys into battle
Send them if you must
But before you make them go there
Make sure the reasons are just

If you think there are reasons for going
And the reasons are worth all the strife
If you think you can pay for the losses – THINK !!!
It's not you who will pay with your life

Think of the wives who'll be widows
Think of the dads who lose sons
Think of the fatherless children
Who are left to be raised by their mums

It's not you who will sit in your kitchen
Feeling the loss on your own
Struggling to think of an answer to
"Mum, when is dad coming home?"

It's not you who will say to your princess
After the plane taxies in
'Your daddy won't walk off to meet you
He's lying inside a coffin'

Think when you have your state dinner
Talking of war, sipping wine
Neither you nor the other state leaders
Are sat in the firing line

If the cause is a just one we'll back you
With great pride in our country we'll fight
But make sure that you know what you're doing
And think 'Is it right? Is It Right?

It's the Thought That Counts

I'm a man. I don't buy presents; I buy petrol, cars and TVs
I don't buy plants, romantic books or shirts that have a sleeve
But it's soon my darling's birthday and it's present time again
And just like Christmas morning, all my efforts are in vain

I've tried so hard these past ten years, to think of something nice
Thinking bigger, thinking multiples, I've paid a higher price
At birthdays and at Christmas special ops I have to mount
I've tried to think of everything but it's *the thought that counts*

I thought she might like clothing. Something special, black and chic
But every time I try this she stops talking for a week
If style is right, the colour's wrong. If the colour's right, it's frumpy
Or it doesn't match her coat and purse so she gets a little grumpy

I bought her diamond earrings and she had a little pout
I had to call her mother as I couldn't work it out
An arctic blast came down the line the telling off was fierce
"Ten years you've know my daughter and her ears are never
pierced!!!"

The heart shaped box of chocolates set her all aglow
A metre wide with gold relief and tied up in a bow
But when I picked the flavours I forgot her allergies
The treat was loved by everyone at the local A&E

I thought a dozen roses might turn her heart to song
With a dozen, dozen roses I could surely not go wrong
It wasn't pollen season and I didn't let them slump
But because of all the aphids they only ever saw the dump

Make up is a thing gals like; mascara, lippy, nails
I bought a set of everything from someone in the sales
High as a kite I got one right but I came down with a crash
Ever since that birthday she has had to hide a nasty rash

I've tried every kind of present. Thought of every kind of gift
I thought I'd make her happy, but I only make her miffed
She swung a punch. She thought I'd duck. A defence I didn't mount
I came to on the kitchen floor and heard
'It's the thought that counts'

The Tick

My parents match. Their eggs all hatch
My early age, dubbed nymph stage

Do what I should till adulthood
Then all sedate, I sit and wait

Poor host passes, jump from grasses
Then find some skin, bury head in

It's intended to get distended
I suck and wait as I inflate

Draw from the beast a rich blood feast
I charge no fees for the Lyme disease

I then detach to find a match
Some adult play, some eggs to lay

After we match our eggs all hatch
End of my reign, it starts again

The tick – a vampire solution from evolution
Or just something odd from a benevolent god?

The Unknown Truth

It's a time of sweet joy when a man not a boy
Says to his kith and his kin
I've learnt what I could, some bad and some good
The next stage has got to begin

Memory lane is a street on which I shall meet
Adventures and friends good and true
As I stand at this end how can I comprehend
The many great things I'll live through

There will be times up ahead some I will dread
Some places I'll not want to dwell
It's time now to roam, to find my new home
And live stories that I'll want to tell

It was good where I've been as baby and teen
But I must say goodbye to my youth
I'll take what I know and forward I'll go
Into the unknown truth

The Ultimate Box of Chocolates

I've got a big box of dark chocolates
They are gooey and tasty and nice
I take all that I want which is greedy
And I simply ignore the high price

I don't pass the box to my children
And my grandkids can suck on a leaf
I won't share the box till it's empty
They're all mine, that's my honest belief

You might think I am selfish and stingy
Well that's simply your warped point of view
I want to be lazy and greedy
And I don't give a hoot about you

That's hardly a positive view point
When kids do it we tell them it's wrong
We train them to care about others
In nursery we teach it with songs

Swap the box for the world that we live in
And the chocolates for coal, oil and gas
The kids and the grandkids as always
Are the ones to whom all this will pass

We use fossil fuels with abandon
It is wasted and frittered away
With nothing to pass to our grandkids
In five decades just what will we say?

There's no value in saying "I'm sorry"
Regret doesn't fill seams with coal
Are fumes what we'll give to the future
And some ashes and empty well holes

If it's wrong to eat all the chocolates
And the greed makes you want to recoil
Then it's wrong to squander resources
And burn all the coal, gas and oil

So let's try to curb our behaviour
Let's resist the lazy temptation
Let's be led by our need, not led by our greed
So there's some for the next generation

Walking the Dog?

I have to walk my doggie. It really is a pain because
It's cold when it is blowy and wet if there is rain
He wanders off if I'm too slow, but hates it on the lead
He always finds the wet bits and stinks of rotting leaves

I try the bike he's still too fast; this dog is full of beans
Don't get a Cocker Spaniel 'cause running's in their genes
I think there is a solution. My best idea by far
Don't take him out for walkies, but go driving in the car

A long straight road, the way is clear, I open up the door
He's up to half the speed of sound before he hits the floor
I jump back in. I hit the gas, somehow the little rotter
Is half a mile along the road and wet from finding water

The race is on. He's near light speed. What tends to slow him down
His great big, floppy, hairy ears, for which spaniels are renowned
Gear 1, gear 2, gear 3, gear 4. I just can't catch him up
I'm sure this little tinker is at least half soyuz pup

He stops to pee, I just sail past, which you might think is wrong
My lead is now extensive, but it doesn't last for long
His ears flip flop, his tongue is out, his tiny legs do strain
And in half a nano-second he's overtaken me again

44

I only give him dog food, from a bag or from a tin
Is there a nuclear reactor hiding underneath his skin?
Or buried in the wavy hair, that grows along his back
This spaniel is assisted by a doggie sized jet pack

Through guilt I stop and let him in the boot to have a rest
I hope this isn't bad for him and he ends up over stressed
But looking at his smiling face, it seems to me quite plain
His eyes look back and plead to me *"Let's do it all again"*

Up or Down - Who Cares?

I can't get all that worked up as the issue's rather small
I think I'm just like any man I don't consider it at all
But you women get so worked up and it always makes you frown
About the petty issue, should the seat be up or down?

It's a toilet seat for goodness sake, two positions by design
If I want it up and it is down, I don't have a little whine
I change the seat position and when my work's complete
I wash my hands and wander out. I don't worry 'bout the seat

Or if I need it level but it's pointing in the air
I move it horizontal so I can use it like a chair
I don't have to think about it. I don't have to make a fuss
And it's not a major issue, which I feel I should discuss

Believe you me if you get it wrong it isn't very nice
It happened once when I was young. I'll never do that twice
So that's the matter over. I don't want the third degree
Just simply check the toilet seat, before you have a pee

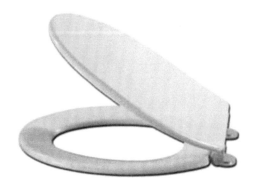

The Weekend

The weathers foul. The air is cold. It's a windy stormy day
But Saturday perfection means in bed is where I stay
No early morning meetings and the kids are not at school
My dreams are shattered by the words "**Can we go to the pool?**"

I pretend that I don't hear them then pretend I have the flu
The wife says '**Just get going. I've got house work still to do**'
I hate the Leisure Centre, with their weekend 'family swim'
You've got to get there early or you probably won't get in

I park the car and still outside, before the pool is seen
My nose detects the dreadful use of way too much chlorine
I queue to pay them money then approach the changing rooms
And every step is closer to the choking chlorine fumes

I get undressed and pack the bags and then I have to prise
The whole lot in a locker that's exactly half their size
Brute force and subtle swearing, then every blessed time
I have to haul it out again, I forgot it needs a dime

Water beckons, the kiddies scream, with joy they all abound
We exit to the waterside and the cacophony of sound
Screaming, splashing, jumping, the noise never dies away
From every wall and ceiling the sounds just ricochet

I test the water with a toe and 'baltic' springs to mind
To enter any further I am rather disinclined
I see my kids immerse themselves all radiating glee
They haven't read the news reports on how much water's in the pee

I venture in. It's frigid but then quicker than a flash
A teenage kid dive bombing makes a really massive splash
Water in my nose and eyes, I want to keep my grace
My kids join in and others too *I HATE SPLASHING ON MY FACE*

The wave machine gets going. I am jostled up and down
Mis-time a jump, breathe-in the surf and you can nearly drown
I chuck my son into the swell he's pretending he's a missile
I caution from the life guard, the control freak with a whistle

I try to stay all happy but it always ends in gloom
The lifeguards now have opened all the different kinds of flume
I don't mind before you use them there are fifteen hundred stairs
But when I hit the water my suit's shoved up my derrière

Once swim suit is extricated I begin to realise
There's a burning red sensation appearing in my eyes
Too much chlorine in the water is surely just a waste
And while we're on the subject, I also hate the taste

I've lost my cool and out we get. The shower could be hotter
And ironically we're in the pool but the nozzle dribbles water
We have a wash with trickle flow and it comes as no surprise
Both kids and I are screaming as there's shampoo in our eyes

Changing room then follows and it's a certain bet
I drop my shirt and trousers, they both get soaking wet
With dripping clothes I help the kids; it's nothing but a fight
Why does the wife dress all the kids in clothing that's skin tight?

Before we leave there's hair to do, it's a tangled soggy mess
There's tears again. It's pain for them and for me it is the stress
Tarantino would be happy by the carnage of the scene
And once again I blame it all on way too much chlorine

So that was fun, it's over now the kids have had their treat
My lie-in comes tomorrow. It will be extra, extra sweet
**'Guess what dear, my parents rang. They booked lunch and I
agreed it'**
With heavy heart I ponder *'Where's the chlorine when I need it?'*

What's Your Special Day?

There's a time late December, a very special date
It only comes but once a year but boy it's worth the wait

A special time, a happy time an invincible soirée
There's not a time that beats it of course it's Boxing Day

Boxing, Boxing, Boxing day oh isn't it divine?
Because it's close to Christmas you've still got lots of wine

No present expectation, Santa Clause has bin
No late night stocking filling and the chance to just lie in

No need to pull a sicky as it's still a holiday
And if you've sadly got to work you should get double pay

You've had to host Godzilla and an irate Genghis khan
But Christmas day is over and the in-laws have moved on

The larder's overflowing, the fridge is full of meat
And ingratiating neighbours means there's lots of chocolate
treats

The stress is gone, the TV's great, the jigsaw's nearly done
The Yuletide strain is over but you've still got all the fun

Some love Christmas morning for others Hogmanay
But don't overlook the magic that's around on Boxing day

When I'm 92

Sometimes I sit and wonder if today will be the day
That you will write a letter or simply call and say
The feelings that you have for me are both simple and profound
That I am someone special you would like to have around

I got your lovely present for my birthday, thanks so much
And the simple little messages when you can keep in touch
You send your care and kisses, but silence then ensues
I have trouble understanding the mixed messages from you

We've talked for many hours, like soul mates we converse
But this doesn't make it better, it only makes it worse
Cause it makes my feelings stronger and I feel the same from you
But the silence makes me wonder which narrative is true

Love is like a mountain, a daunting thing to climb
Is waiting for your love to show a simple waste of time?
I have tenderness inside me and I hope that it is plain
To you it is directed, but is this hope in vain?

As we live life we need a hand, to help us in bad times
Maybe if we're close enough you'd consider holding mine
Life is never perfect, but it's more perfect next to you
Will it be your hand I'm holding when I am 92?

The Yuletide Rush is Over

The Yuletide rush is over
All the decorations up
Gifts lie in-wait to meet their fate
There's mulled wine in the cup

The shopping once torrential flow
Has dwindled to a trickle
We once did hold a pot of gold
But we're left with just a nickel

Our cards long gone (at least we hope)
And the ones received on show
The written gift from friends adrift
Displayed in jumbled rows

No matter what it looked like bare
The tree is now pristine
With baubles bright and flashing light
How lovely does it gleam

The turkeys donned its Christmas pose
Lying flat out on the rack
The guests are here with much good cheer
And all their bags unpacked

We want some snow on Christmas Eve
To fall throughout the night
We kneel and pray so at break of day
There's a blanket of pure white

There's little else for us to do
For Santa we must wait
With lots of toys and Christmas joys
So we hope he isn't late

A calm descends on Christmas Eve
After all that we did cram
We have a treat and raise our feet
And sip a warming dram

How glorious is this annual lull
After weeks of Christmas rush
When life slows down we rest our crown
There's a tranquil placid hush

We sit relax and raise a glass
To the preparations done
And go to bed with happy head
To await the Christmas fun

You Don't Get to the Moon Watching Soaps

Great people have walked us thru history and
Their footprint prints still lead the advance
Did they all work hard to achieve this
Or succeed in a soap opera trance?

Columbus, Sir Francis, De Gama
Centuries later we still tell their tale
Will that be said about Crossroads
Coronation Street or Emmerdale?

Would Hepburn or Dietrich or Garbo
Have an instantly recognized face
If every week they watched Dallas
Knots Landing or perhaps Peyton Place?

Gutenberg invented the print press
Chuck Yeager went faster than sound
As kids if I wanted to find them
Is the TV where they could be found?

Did the father of Newton or Turing
Archimedes or Galilei
Say stop what you're learning come running
A cheap drama I want you to see?

Bronte and Shelly and Atwood
Great footprints in history have won
Was life or some Eastender antics
The source of their inspiration?

Bannister, Ali, Jess Owen
George Washington, and J-F-K
Da Vinci, Cézanne and Picasso
Seuss, Tolkien, Shakespeare, Zane Grey

Presley, The Beatles, or Streisand
Versace, Chanel and Dior
If talking up soaps at the table
Would all be a dinner guest bore

Socrates, Plato, Aristotle
For thousands of years have been read
Who's gonna remember soap writers
A thousand years after there're dead?

Wilberforce, Lincoln, Mandela
I think you would have to agree
Their work was not driven by someone
From a soap seen on tea time TV

The wheel, logarithms, the Bronze age
The web, penicillin, the phone
Grand opera, concertos by Mozart
Or life changing sculptures in stone

Ramses, Alfred, Alexander
In history are known as 'The Great'
Their fame wasn't built on soap operas
From the UK or United States

I'm sure at the birth of Neil Armstrong
For success both his parents had hopes
Neil said he took just a small step
But it wasn't achieved watching soaps

The scrap heap of history is bulging
It is soap scripts and lethargy strewn
But Neil didn't care to watch TV
And his footprints are seen on the moon